MCPHERSON'S SPORTS & FITNESS MANUAL

John McPherson

Zondervan Publishing House

Grand Rapids, Michigan

A Division of HarperCollins*Publishers*

McPherson's Sports and Fitness Manual
Copyright © 1993 by John McPherson
ISBN 0-310-61431-7

Requests for information should be addressed to
Zondervan Publishing House
Grand Rapids, Michigan 49530

Printed in the United States of America

93 94 95 96 97 98 99 00 / ML / 10 9 8 7 6 5 4 3 2 1

For Dad,
who taught me
how to catch,
throw,
and warm the bench
with dignity

Coach Wazler discovered that attaching likenesses of players' mothers-in-law to the blocking sleds is a powerful motivational tool.

"Okay, now the left nostril. Good!"

At a track meet in New Jersey

Although they did help to boost attendance at tournaments, the PGA cheerleaders were eventually banned from the tour after repeated complaints from players.

Bob Swilnard was a lifeguard with an attitude.

"I guess maybe *now* my canine-ankle-fences
don't look so stupid, huh, wise guy?"

Bud Skuzkowski's technique of not showering during wrestling season led him to fourteen straight victories.

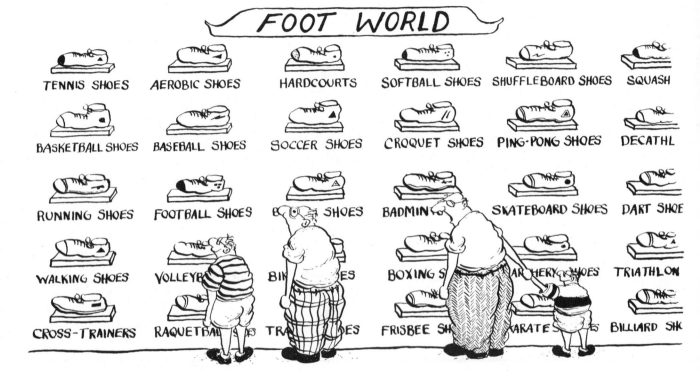

"Remember the good old days when they were all just called 'sneakers'?"

"Worst slice I ever saw!"

Jack Mangiante wasn't about to let another
grounder roll through his legs.

"For Pete's sake, watch where you're going!
A foot more to the left and you would have
put a ski right through my new curtains!"

Hockey in heaven

Joe Halm's fateful "cannonball"
would go down in Silver Bay YMCA history.

Track Coach Verne Pestwell knew it was
important that his runners stretch out
before each meet.

Although half of the team was out with the flu, the Fighting Pigeons of Varnberg State did their best to make their opponents think they were at full strength.

"I lost my whistle."

"I thought the family-rental rate was too good
to be true."

"Cotton candy?! You traded your *glove* for some cotton candy?!!"

Despite an 0-and-14 season and slumping attendance,
loyal Pigeon fans still showed their
support by doing the wave.

"I think we better have a little talk with
Wilson after the meet."

"I don't like the looks of this storm."

"Hey, can they do that?!"

The Dembrosky brothers weren't about to let the fact that they live in Kansas keep them from experiencing the thrills of surfing.

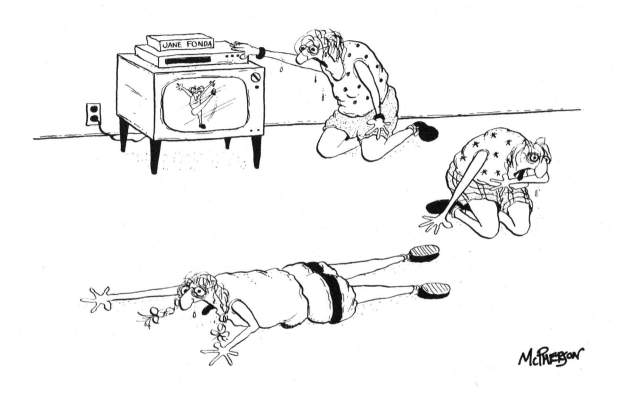

"Here's the problem! The workout tape has been on fast-forward the whole time!"

How to make your wife hysterical

In a play unprecedented in league history,
Chip Comstock misreads the third-base coach's signals
and steal pitcher's mound.

"You better get those bindings checked out when you get back to the lodge. Those things should have released after a wipe-out like this."

Coach Finkler was a desperate man.

"How's Brian doin'? Is he still up?"

As a courtesy to their fellow competitors, more and more runners are wearing mudflaps.

"Bummer."

"I don't care if the school did get an incredible deal by buying this thing secondhand from 'Wacky World'; it still gives me the creeps."

"You really ought to try one of these new
wide-body rackets."

The Puzney College Wombats were undefeated
since they got their new uniforms.

Aerobics for couch potatoes

"Coach is pretty serious about keeping any
pass-rushers from getting through
the offensive line."

By marking the volleyball with red paint,
referees at Pilburn College were able
to avoid heated disputes over line calls.

"I realize this may affect your playing, but those darned squeaky sneakers drive me nuts."

Dale's .026 batting average was well-known
throughout the league.

The Spatney State Gophers finally learned
the truth about the throngs of fans that had been
showing up at their games.

"Hey! You're right! They *are* big jelly beans!"

"This ticket here is from Stowe in late March of '79. Great spring conditions that day."

"Slow down! SLOW DOWN!"

Dan just wasn't working out as a spotter
for the gymnastics team.

Just when he was on the verge of losing the match,
Brad took out the rubber hand that had been
hidden in his suit.

Joanne and Peggy were pretty impressed with
Joe's surfing abilities, until the tide receded.

"Personally, I don't have a whole lot of confidence in our cheerleaders."

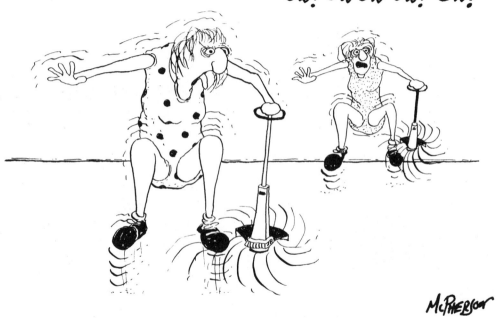

Those who have mastered high-speed jump-roping
have turned to the latest aerobic fad: weedeater jumping.

"I'm saving up to buy some skis."

"Hold it! Nobody move! I just lost a contact!"

"Hey, six against five! No fair!"

A lot of people felt that Stella didn't have
the self-confidence needed to be a top gymnast.

"Management says they're fed up with losing
foul balls and homers to the fans."

"Wow, man, you shouldn't have tried
to lift so much."

Having lost twenty consecutive games, Coach Comstock
did his best to help the team regain its confidence.

"Let's have a round of applause for Lloyd Millman, winner of our handball tournament for the sixth year in a row."

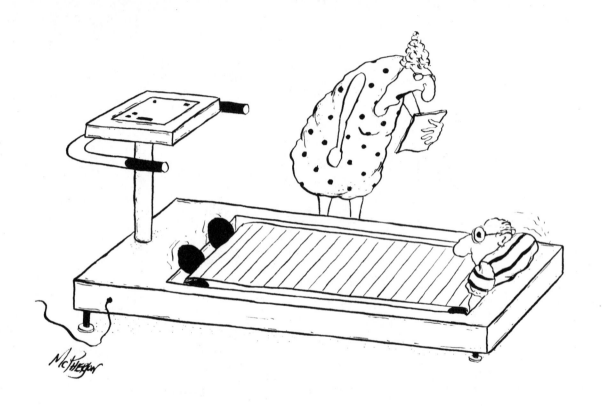

"Here you go, right on page 13 of the manual:
'*Never* stop walking while the treadmill is on.'"

Ron saw himself as a pioneer in
the sport of boatless waterskiing.

"For cryin' out loud, turn it down! TURN IT DOWN!"

Despite months of practice, the Mielke State
relay team hadn't quite perfected their hand-offs.

Although all of the players were given uniforms, it didn't take long to figure out which guys weren't going to make the final cuts.

"I'm saving up to get one of those treadmills for jogging."

"Okay! Now, *left* leg kicks! Good! Twenty more! Super!
Okay, now double-time! Perfect!"

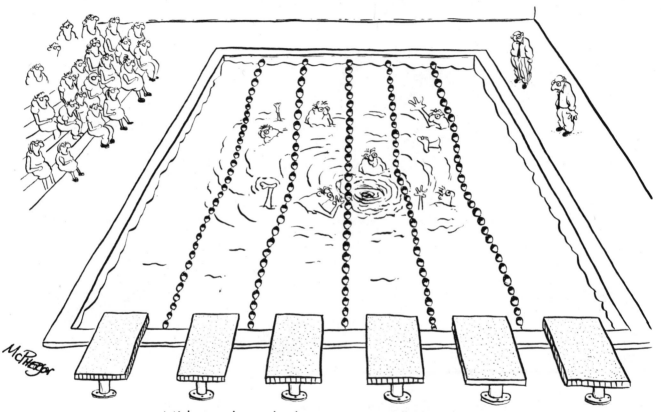

Midway through the 100-meter freestyle, somebody
pulled the plug.

"Before we start practice today I want to apologize for the little mix-up we've had with the uniforms. I'll be talking to the ballet instructor tomorrow and hopefully we'll get things cleared up before the big game on Saturday."

Track officials eventually caught on to Coach Wazman and
banned him from all meets, but not before his high-jumpers
set fourteen consecutive state records.

Initially intended to provide added protection,
the team's new inflatable uniforms were also
effective in intimidating their opponents.

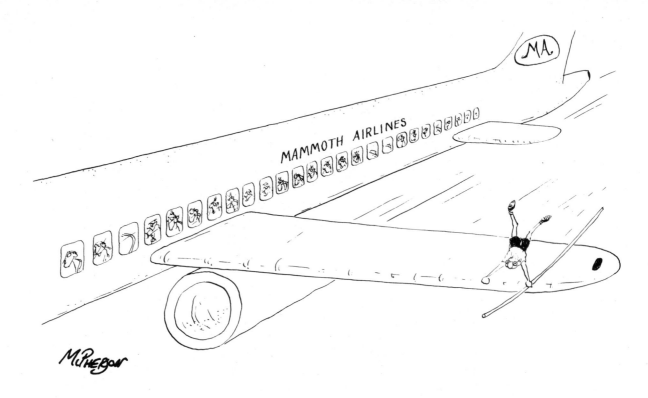

Unfortunately, Ronnie Klingburn was not available
to receive his medal for placing first
in the pole-vaulting competition.

Even though they were hard to run in,
Mike's new shoes made him a serious base-stealing threat.

The latest trend in beach wear: Pontoon shoes.

"High jump?! I thought this was a limbo contest!!"

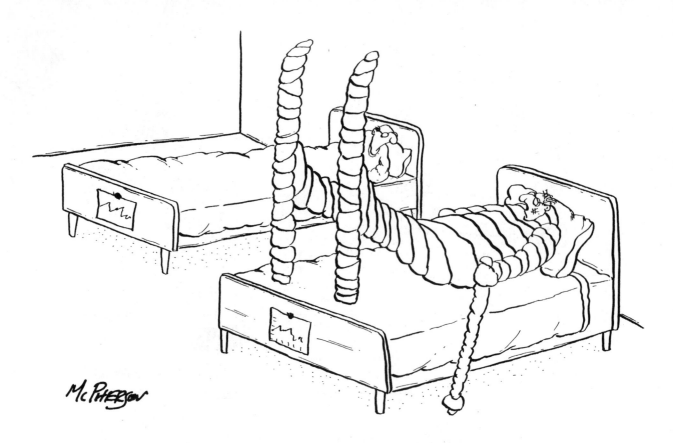

"Me? A skiing accident."

"This is our top-of-the-line exercise bike, for total biking realism, complete with a barking dog, a built-in tape deck that plays a recording of rude comments from motorists, and this nozzle that emits a fine mist of bugs."

The dreaded return trip from the stadium snack bar.

There are times when being a whiz at math
can be a definite drawback.

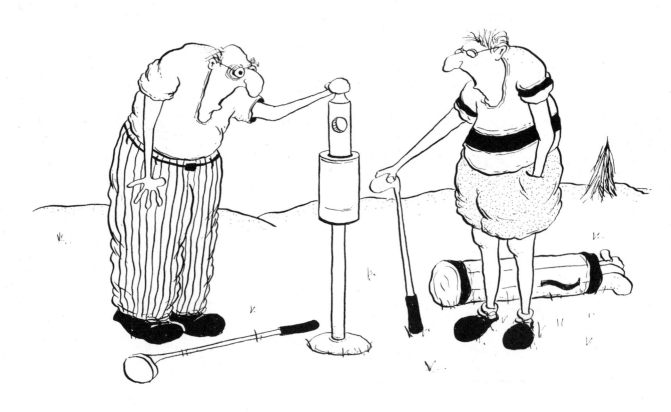

"It doesn't matter that you lost it in the ball washer.
You still lost your ball. That's a one-stroke penalty."

Though he was a star on the soccer team,
Les Babko was having a tough time with baseball.

"According to the on-board calorie computer, you burned the equivalent of three M&Ms."

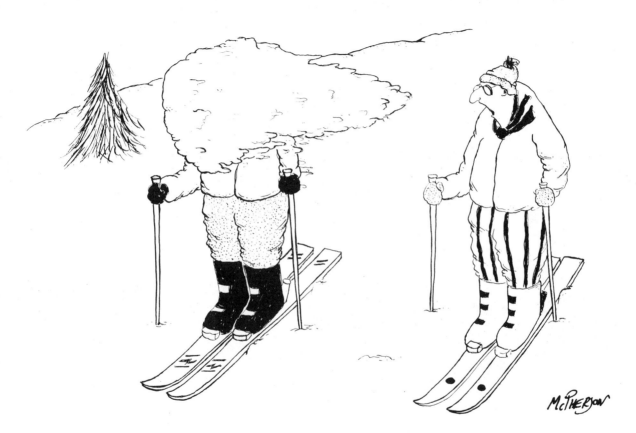

"Sorry. I should have warned you that that snow gun was coming up."

A hot new fad: The party skateboard

Research has shown that wearing a baseball cap backward lowers one's IQ by as much as 50 points.

THUNK!

"Whoa! Tough serve!"

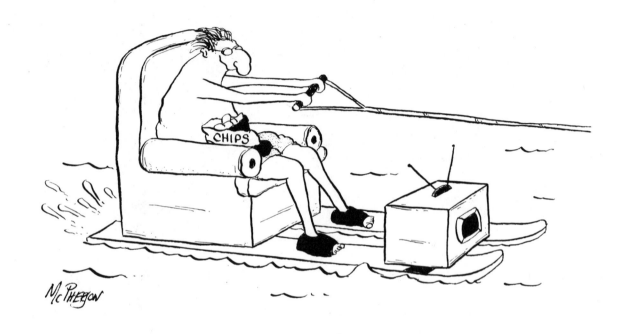

Laziness was a driving force in all aspects
of Wayne's life.

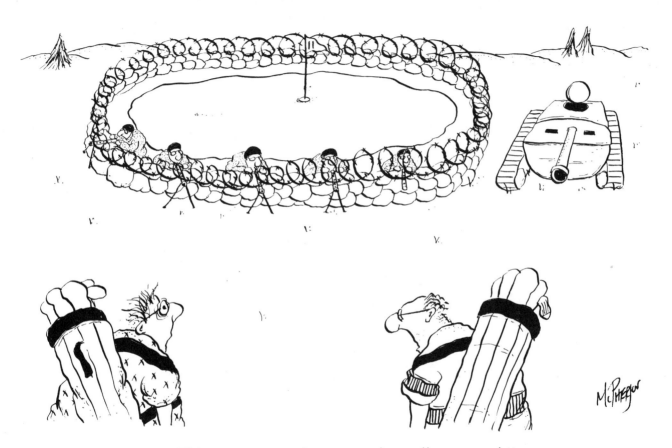

"This next green is extremely well-protected."

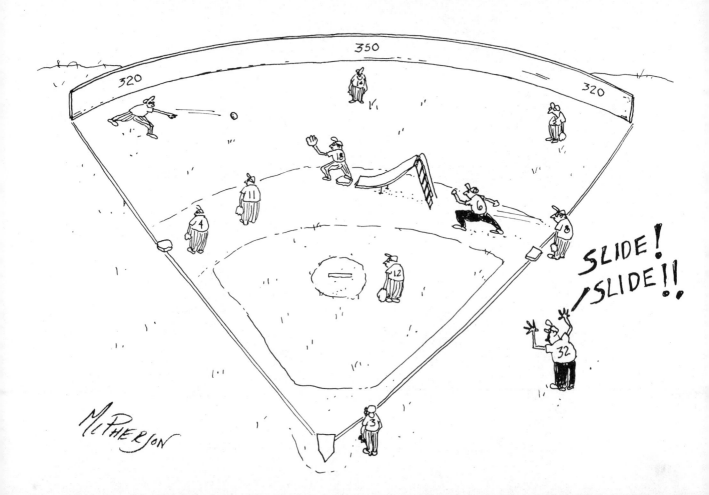

Dwayne was starting to reconsider his decision
to be water boy for the cross-country team.

"'Tape' is just what they call the finish line.
You weren't supposed to use *real* tape!!"

Although Linda Waxgard had set a new school record, an observant official spotted a possible violation.

CLOMP!

"I just figured, hey, why spend a fortune on a
set of yuppie-looking wrist- and ankle-weights?"

After hitting seven consecutive shots into the
water hazard, Rick began to show a hint of apathy
toward his golf game.

Always the practical jokers, track officials substituted a bungee cord for the finish line in the men's 400 meter.

"Wilson, follow the blockers up the middle, then cut right and make a break for the snack bar. If we get strong blocking out there, we just might get our food back here before half-time is over."

"What the heck kind of wax are you using?"

Unfortunately for Dominique, neither the super-stepper nor the accompanying cassette tape was refundable.

"Okay, let me get this straight, kid. You're betting us fifty bucks that you can slam-dunk the ball on the first try, *and* you're going to do it left-handed?! You're on!"

Suddenly it dawned on Ed why he felt like he had
such an incredible lead on the other runners."

"Have you ever thought about maybe getting
your racket restrung?"

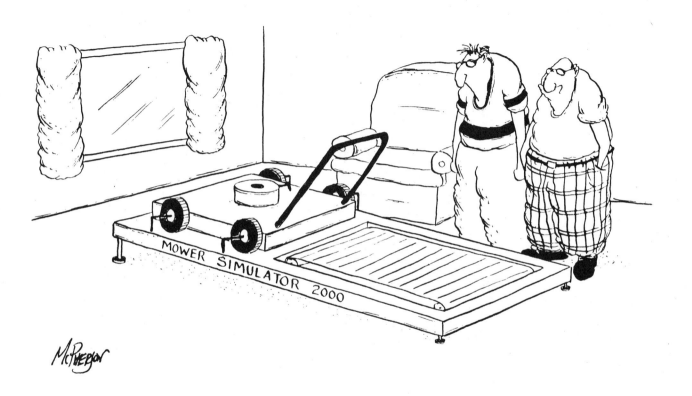

Wayne's dad thought the new mower simulator would be
a great way to keep Wayne in shape between mowings.

Ed looked forward to the day when he'd be able to get down the slope without training-skis.

Trailing by 26 with only 57 seconds left,
Falmut State was starting to get desperate.

Track-and-field practical jokes

"It's the only number under a hundred
that the team hasn't retired."

The '90s dad: Able to spend time with his kids while still indulging in his favorite sport.

"Whoa! Great shot! Okay, now see if you can nail
Mr. Wazney, getting into the red Trans Am, third row!"

One of the drawbacks of wearing cleats.

"Boy, that was something! I don't know who was more
surprised, you or that deer!"

"You want it set on low, high, or industrial strength?"

In an attempt to liven up what they consider to be a slow-moving game, Phil and his friends created full-contact golf.

A couple of near misses by the Wormsley High
javelin team had caused school officials to take some
safety precautions.